HOW TO LET GO OF PAST TRAUMA AND MAKE PEACE WITH YOURSELF

A Guide On How To Forgive And Let Go Of Past Hurts, Enjoy

Emotional Freedom, Stop Overthinking And Rumination, Create a

Beautiful Life Again

JORDAN ROSE

CONTENTS

THANKS FOR YOUR PURCHASE

INTRODUCTION

In the quiet parts of our minds, we carry memories—some good, some really hard. This book, "How To Let Go Of Past Trauma and Make Peace With Yourself," is like a friend helping you through tough times. It's not a rulebook but a guide to heal, forgive, and find peace inside yourself.

Let me tell you a bit about why I wrote this. There was a time in my life when old hurts weighed me down. It felt like I couldn't enjoy the present because my mind was stuck in the past, always overthinking and going in circles.

I figured things out not by doing something big but by realizing it's okay to feel vulnerable. That's what started my healing journey, and I want to share what I learned with you. This book isn't a quick fix; it's about looking inside yourself. We'll talk about forgiveness, a powerful way to let go of anger and feel free. With simple activities, stories, and useful tips, I hope to help you on your journey to let go of the past and find peace.

This book isn't about erasing what happened but changing how we see it. We can grow stronger, even when things were tough. It's about seeing that, no matter how hard it was, we have the power to turn our stories into ones of strength and triumph. "How To Let Go Of

Past Trauma and Make Peace With Yourself" is like a friendly guide, helping you discover yourself, understand your feelings, and feel strong again.

As we go through this journey together, I ask you to keep an open heart and be ready to feel a bit vulnerable. It might be tough sometimes, but facing our fears and dealing with the past is how we find real change. This book is more than just advice—it's a reminder that we all have the power to heal, no matter how deep the hurt.

You are welcome my dear reader!

CHAPTER 1

THE IMPACT OF TOUGH TIMES

Life is like a rollercoaster, with its ups and downs. Sometimes, we go through tough times that leave lasting marks on us. These challenging experiences, known as trauma, can have a profound impact on how we live our lives today.

Firstly, let's understand what trauma means. Trauma is not just physical injuries; it's also about emotional wounds. It's like having a big emotional bruise inside us. Trauma can happen when we go through really hard and scary things, like accidents, loss of loved ones, or even bullying.

The Memory Game

One way trauma influences our present is through memories. Imagine your brain is like a giant filing cabinet, storing all your memories. Traumatic events can become like those stubborn files that never seem to go away. When something reminds us of the tough times we've been through, those memories can come rushing back, making us feel sad, scared, or angry all over again.

The Body's Alarm System

Our bodies have a built-in alarm system called "fight or flight." It's like having a superhero inside us that helps us deal with danger. When we've been through trauma, our superhero can get a bit too sensitive. Imagine if your alarm went off every time a leaf fell from a tree – it would be pretty annoying, right? That's what happens with our bodies after trauma. Little things can make our alarm go off, making us feel on edge or jumpy even when there's no real danger.

Changing How We See the World

Trauma can also change how we see the world. Imagine wearing glasses that make everything look gloomy and scary. That's a bit like how trauma can affect our perspective. When we've been through tough times, we might start expecting bad things to happen all the time. It's like our brains put on those gloomy glasses, making it hard to see the good stuff around us.

Building Walls Around Our Hearts

Another way trauma influences our present is by making us build walls around our hearts. Imagine your heart is a cozy home. When we go through really hard times, we might try to protect ourselves by putting up walls. These walls can make it difficult for others to get close to us. We might be afraid of getting hurt again, so we keep people at a distance. While these walls might feel like protection, they can also keep out the warmth and love that others want to share.

The Ripple Effect on Relationships

Trauma can create ripples in our relationships. It's like throwing a pebble into a pond – the ripples spread out and touch everything around them. When we've been through tough times, it can be hard to trust others. We might worry that people will leave us or hurt us, so we keep our guard up. This can make it challenging to form deep connections with others, even if they want to be there for us.

Coping Mechanisms: Friends or Foes?

To deal with the pain of trauma, we might develop coping mechanisms – ways to help us feel better. It's like having a trusty sidekick to support us through tough times. But sometimes, these coping mechanisms can become like tricky friends. For example, if we use things like food, video games, or staying busy all the time to avoid thinking about the tough stuff, these friends might start causing more harm than good.

BREAKING FREE: HEALING FROM TRAUMA

Trauma can cast a long shadow over our lives, but it doesn't have to be the final chapter of our story. Healing from trauma is a journey, a path towards reclaiming our sense of self and rediscovering the beauty of life.

Acknowledging the Pain

The first step to healing is acknowledging the pain. It's like turning on a light in a dark room – we need to see what's there before we can start cleaning up. Acknowledging our pain doesn't mean dwelling on it; it means recognizing that it exists and allowing ourselves to feel the emotions that come with it. It's okay to be sad, angry, or scared. These feelings are like messengers, telling us something needs attention.

Opening Up: Talking About It

One of the most powerful tools for healing is opening up and talking about our experiences. Imagine our emotions are like pieces of a puzzle scattered on the floor. By sharing our story with someone we trust – a friend, family member, or therapist – we begin to pick up those pieces and put them back together. Talking about it is not a sign of weakness; it's a courageous step towards understanding and acceptance.

Seeking Professional Support

Just as we consult experts for physical ailments, seeking professional support for emotional wounds is crucial. A therapist or counselor is like a guide on our healing journey. They provide a safe space to explore our feelings, offer coping strategies, and help us build the resilience needed to face life's challenges. It's okay to ask for help; in fact, it's a sign of strength.

Creating Safe Spaces

Creating safe spaces in our lives is essential for healing. These spaces can be physical, like a cozy corner in our home, or emotional, where we surround ourselves with supportive and understanding people. Safe spaces allow us to express ourselves without judgment, fostering a sense of security and belonging. It's like having a refuge where we can retreat when the world feels overwhelming.

Self-Compassion: Treating Ourselves with Kindness

Healing from trauma involves being kind to ourselves. Imagine if we treated ourselves as we would a dear friend going through a tough time. Self-compassion is like offering a gentle hand to the wounded parts of ourselves, acknowledging that we deserve love and care. It's okay to take breaks, practice self-care, and treat ourselves with the same kindness we extend to others.

Understanding Triggers

Triggers are like landmines, unexpected and powerful. They can bring back intense emotions and memories associated with trauma. Understanding our triggers is a crucial aspect of healing. It's like mapping out the terrain and being aware of potential challenges. Once we recognize our triggers, we can develop coping mechanisms to navigate them and prevent them from derailing our progress.

Building Healthy Habits

Healing is not just about addressing the wounds; it's also about building a strong foundation for the future. Building healthy habits is like planting seeds for a flourishing garden. This includes regular exercise, nutritious meals, sufficient sleep, and engaging in activities that bring joy. Healthy habits support our overall well-being and contribute to the resilience needed for the journey ahead.

Cultivating Resilience

Resilience is the ability to bounce back from adversity. Cultivating resilience is like strengthening our emotional muscles. It involves learning from setbacks, adapting to change, and developing a positive mindset. Resilience doesn't mean avoiding challenges but facing them with a newfound strength. By embracing the ups and downs of life, we become better equipped to navigate the twists and turns on our healing journey.

Embracing Growth

Healing from trauma is not just about returning to the person we were before; it's about embracing growth. Imagine a tree that, despite being weathered by storms, continues to reach for the sky. Trauma can be a catalyst for personal growth and transformation. By facing our pain and working through it, we develop a deeper understanding of ourselves and cultivate the resilience to face whatever comes our way.

In the grand story of our lives, trauma is just one chapter. It might leave a mark, but it doesn't have to define the whole story. By understanding how trauma influences our present and taking steps to heal, we can start writing new chapters filled with hope, resilience, and the strength to face whatever comes our way. Life is a journey, and every step we take towards healing brings us closer to a brighter, happier future.

LETTING GO OF PAST MISTAKES

At times, you might do or say things that you wish you hadn't. If you've gone through this recently, you could be finding it hard to forgive yourself, especially if your actions hurt someone dear to you.

A couple of months back, I had a disagreement with a friend. It unfolded like most misunderstandings do: quickly and unexpectedly. I barely had a moment to grasp what was going on.

My friend was urging me to join him in a business venture, and I politely tried to say no. After a bit of back-and-forth, my patience wore thin, and he started to seem less like a friend and more like a persistent salesperson.

He then said something that felt like a personal insult to me. I got angry and reacted without giving it much thought. I believed I was right in my response, but later on, I realized I had misunderstood his words and jumped to conclusions.

Even after a follow-up talk, with all my apologies, I couldn't shake the feeling that I had made a big mistake. I worried that our relationship would never be the same.

That incident in my life got me thinking about how we get stuck on our own mistakes. They can make us feel trapped in the past and shape our future selves.

My personal thoughts and experience resulted in these seven steps to forgiving yourself:

1. Identify your actions.

To forgive yourself, first, understand what you did. Write down the details of what happened and how your actions contributed to the situation. Avoid blaming others or external factors—focus on your own role. It might feel uncomfortable, but embrace this vulnerability with compassion instead of pushing it away.

In my case, I initially justified my actions by pointing out my friend's unusually aggressive behavior. Once I shifted my focus to my own actions, I realized I had rushed to judge his words.

2. Seek forgiveness.

Asking for forgiveness is challenging. It means acknowledging your wrongdoing and expressing remorse. Avoid downplaying your responsibility with phrases like "I'm sorry if..." or "I'm sorry but..." In my situation, I apologized to my friend, admitting my mistake and asking for forgiveness.

3. Forgive yourself when negative thoughts arise.

Even after resolving the issue with my friend, I battled guilt and negative thoughts about my actions. Self-forgiveness is a gradual process, not a one-time event. Each time negative thoughts surfaced, I took a deep breath and let go of the negativity. Find a similar act of kindness for yourself when negativity arises.

4. Show up and be visible.

Dr. Brené Brown's insight on vulnerability inspired this step. Instead of withdrawing after a painful mistake, gather the courage to engage with life. The temptation to avoid interactions due to fear of judgment or reminders of the past is strong. I hesitated to face my friend, fearing judgment, but when I showed up, my fears were unfounded.

If showing up is challenging, recognize that you've gained wisdom that can help future relationships thrive if you have the strength to try again.

5. Appreciate your mistakes.

Express gratitude for your mistakes, even the embarrassing and painful ones. Reflect on how these experiences changed you—did they make you wiser, stronger, or more discerning? I learned the risks of a quick temper and hasty judgment. Now, when upset, I give myself time to reflect. I'm thankful for the chance to grow in these areas. If you can see your mistakes as opportunities to grow, you can be grateful for them too.

6. Wholeheartedly love every part of yourself.

Joseph Campbell once said, "The privilege of a lifetime is being who you are." Embrace that privilege; be who you are now, not who you used to be. Take pride in the person you've become, despite, or perhaps because of, your past mistakes.

My own errors and imperfections have contributed to making me a better friend. Embracing all aspects of yourself, including your past mistakes, will only make you more resilient and robust.

You Deserve Forgiveness

These steps may not always be simple, especially when we've truly messed up. Yet, we can bounce back from our mistakes, learn from them, forgive ourselves, and move forward.

You deserve your own love and forgiveness. Believe in this wholeheartedly.

Make a commitment to practice these steps daily, even on those days when it feels challenging.

Decide to forgive yourself. Decide to let go of the past. Decide to live in the present. Look toward the future with hope and optimism.

HOW TO FORGIVE WHEN YOU DON'T WANT TO

Similar to countless other women, my relationship with my mother was intricate and often strained. Despite living thousands of miles away, a mere email or phone call could easily agitate me.

Visits became tense, nerve-wracking encounters where I found myself dissecting every word she uttered, searching for potential passive-aggressive undertones that could spark an argument.

For years, I received a lot of advice on how to forgive, but none of it seemed to resonate:

- Resentment is the poison you feed yourself, hoping someone else will die.

- Forgiveness is a choice.

- Refusing to forgive is living in the past.

Despite understanding the cost of harboring resentment—the constant replaying of old arguments and the anticipation of future conflicts—I struggled to genuinely want to forgive her. This internal resistance was a truth I had avoided acknowledging for a long time.

Admitting that a petty part of ourselves doesn't want to forgive is uncomfortable. We often claim we "don't know how," and while that might be true, the deeper truth is that there's a part of us that doesn't want to forgive.

We resist acknowledging this part because it challenges the stories we tell ourselves—that we're mean, petty, and judgmental. Ironically, when we refuse to forgive, we exhibit mean, petty, and judgmental behaviors.

This isn't intentional. It's a response to the hurt we've experienced, and forgiveness can feel like excusing or condoning the actions that caused the pain. There's an irrational fear that forgiving someone implies acceptance of their actions, and we worry they might repeat them.

However, whether or not we forgive has no bearing on controlling another person's behavior. People act as they will. The only person we release by forgiving is ourselves, freeing ourselves from the burden of monitoring someone else's actions or dwelling on the past.

So, how can you navigate the process of forgiving others?

These steps aren't inherently easy, especially as many work together, but they form the intricate pieces that compose the whole.

First, recognize the parts of yourself that resist forgiveness.

Identify the aspects that derive a sense of power from withholding forgiveness, acknowledging these rather than pushing them away. It's a sign of personal growth to be aware of these aspects.

Second, examine the stories associated with your reluctance to forgive.

Commonly, there's a fear that forgiveness implies absolution from responsibility for someone's actions. Understand that when someone wrongs another, they suffer, whether consciously or unconsciously. Acknowledge this suffering, even if they don't express it overtly.

Third, seek common ground.

Find similarities between yourself and the person you're reluctant to forgive. It might be challenging, but understanding that you share common human experiences, including moments of deceit or fear, can pave the way for compassion and release.

Finally, realize that a lack of forgiveness stems from a lack of boundaries.

Recognize that forgiving doesn't mean allowing the same actions to recur. Decide what behaviors, dynamics, and beliefs you won't tolerate in your life. Establish clear boundaries and assert them with compassion, understanding that others' unkindness often stems from their own suffering.

The key is not revenge or retaliation but setting and maintaining healthy boundaries. When you decide what you won't tolerate and remain firm in your choices, the fear of a repeat occurrence diminishes.

In a pivotal moment for me, stuck in traffic, I realized I had the power to decide who I am concerning forgiving my mother. I understood that my life was what I chose it to be, and a painful relationship with her didn't need to be a part of it. All I wanted was to love her, grateful for the life and lessons she provided.

Before experiencing deep forgiveness, I sought guidance from various therapists. The simplicity and elegance of this moment would have seemed impossible then. However, it holds true: "Freedom is what we do with what's been done to us." Our circumstances don't define us; our choices in response to them do.

CHAPTER 2

LETTING GO OF RESENTMENT

"Can I kiss you?" he asked.

I wasn't really keen on kissing him, but it had been a decent first date, and I didn't want to hurt his feelings by saying no. We stood by my car in broad daylight, and I thought, what harm could it do? So, with little enthusiasm, I nodded.

He, however, was more excited than I expected. As he leaned in, I closed my eyes, endured the kiss that didn't exactly set my toes tingling, and it went on longer than I'd wanted. Again, I didn't know how to end it without hurting his feelings, so I waited. After enduring a second, even longer, and less-desired kiss, I finally managed to extricate myself, thanked him for lunch, slipped into my car, and drove away.

I was relieved to be done with the date, and honestly, I was annoyed—no, scratch that, I was resentful. This perfectly nice man had now taken on an unpleasant aura in my mind. Couldn't he see I wasn't interested? Why did he have to pull me into a second kiss? Oh, how I resented him!

As I delved into the world of online dating in search of a life partner, scenarios like this repeated themselves. After a staggering fifty-seven first dates in two-and-a-half years, I came to believe that dating, if approached with self-examination, can be a tremendous route to self-growth.

One valuable lesson from my quest for a life partner was realizing the importance of setting clear limits before leaving for a date. Before gaining this clarity, I became very familiar with the emotion of resentment.

In a moment of resentment toward a thoughtful, considerate man, I had an epiphany. He had gone a bit further than I wanted, but he had done nothing wrong. He would have backed off if I had asked. My resentment was misplaced, and the real source of my anger was myself.

This realization was a turning point. Resentment isn't anger with someone else; it's anger with oneself, misdirected at someone else through the lens of victimhood.

Everything changed. As a former people-pleaser, setting clear limits was challenging. It was easier to go with the flow and then blame my dates when my true wishes weren't honored. But playing the victim didn't lead to happiness or empowerment.

Acknowledging my role in creating boundaries, and taking responsibility for my desires, allowed me to release resentment and make the necessary changes. Setting clear boundaries became a tool for a happier life, not just in dating but in all areas.

Resentment is anger with oneself, misdirected at someone else through the lens of victimhood. This simple statement became my mantra, guiding me to a less turbulent path through my dating days.

Knowing something and consistently integrating it into your life are two different things. Recently, I discovered the need to remind myself of my epiphany about resentment.

The considerate and wonderful man I mentioned earlier is now my life partner for over three years. However, he doesn't share my interest in physical exercise, unlike me, who places a higher value on fitness. But even with this difference, I don't always achieve my goal of daily exercise.

In a psychology class, I learned that low physical fitness can be "contagious." Studies indicate that people are more likely to adopt sedentary or obese habits when those in their close social network exhibit similar behaviors. I stumbled upon this data when I felt frustrated about work interfering with my exercise routine.

I found it tempting to resent my partner for not being a workout companion. It seemed easier to blame him than to acknowledge my own shortcomings. However, I quickly remembered my earlier epiphany: Resentment is anger with oneself, misdirected at someone else through the lens of victimhood.

While it might be simpler to go to the gym if my partner shared my enthusiasm, the responsibility for my lack of exercise lies with me. I chose to prioritize work over going to the gym, and any anger directed elsewhere was unproductive.

Phew! I felt like I dodged a bullet. Instead of harboring resentment toward my partner, I felt grateful for the lessons learned during my dating days.

It served as a good reminder, and now I'm on the lookout for any signs of resentment so I can address it before it grows. Whether it's about unwanted kisses or a gym visit, taking full responsibility and recognizing that the anger is internal dissipates resentment and creates space for greater happiness.

THE WAY OUT OF RESENTMENT

Life is short. Wasting time feeling angry or resentful about past events or missed opportunities is counterproductive. Contrary to the belief that such feelings motivate us, they often hinder our quest for fulfillment and happiness.

Accomplishments fueled by resentment seldom contribute to serenity and fulfillment. More importantly, the moments spent in a negative state pass without offering anything positive. They are gone forever.

Resentment acts like a cancer, eating away at time that could be filled with love and joy. Here are four powerful tips to reduce resentment and live a happier life:

Think loving thoughts for the person you resent:

Challenge yourself to send love to someone you resent. Regardless of your beliefs, spend time each day thinking loving thoughts about them, wishing them good fortune and blessings. Verbalize your wishes for them, saying, for example, "May Lisa receive love, health, and peace today." Initially challenging, this practice gradually transforms ill feelings into peace and love.

Check your motives and expectations:

Avoid setting yourself up for resentment by evaluating your motives and expectations. When helping others, ensure you're doing it without expecting something in return. Giving without expectations reduces the likelihood of feeling let down.

Be grateful:

Cultivate gratitude to diminish resentment. Create a gratitude list when feeling stressed or resentful. Write down at least ten things you're grateful for in that moment. Focusing on what you have rather than what you lack diminishes resentment.

Stay open to different outcomes:

Realize that happiness is an inside job, and you already possess what you need to be happy. Avoid placing demands on others or situations. Reducing resentment requires mindfulness and practice, starting with awareness of its manifestations.

Reflecting on a situation where resentment arose, such as helping paint a house unexpectedly, can provide valuable insights. Mindfully acknowledging and removing oneself from the situation, seeking acceptance, guidance, and willingness, can lead to profound realizations about expectations and happiness.

Ultimately, managing expectations and choosing happiness regardless of circumstances are powerful tools for a more content and fulfilling life.

BUILDING EMOTIONAL FREEDOM

"I can't be responsible for your happiness, no matter how much I want you to be happy," were words that brought tears to my eyes, but they also brought an overwhelming sense of freedom. My mother, battling major depressive disorder, had shaped my belief that I could somehow lift her spirits. I strived to be the perfect daughter, suppressing my own emotions to make her smile, only to feel responsible for her sadness.

Internalizing her moods, I lost the ability to distinguish between her feelings and my own. This pattern extended into my relationships, resulting in unhealthy, codependent dynamics. Desiring emotional freedom, a therapist's revelation transformed me: "It's okay to feel angry, sad, disappointed, or frustrated."

This newfound permission to embrace a spectrum of emotions liberated me. Emotional health demanded establishing boundaries, differentiating between my feelings and others', fostering personal responsibility for my emotions. I learned valuable lessons:

Permit Yourself to Feel:

Striving for perpetual happiness is unrealistic. Allow yourself to feel without judgment or analysis. Experience emotions as they come, patiently and compassionately.

Identify Your Emotions:

Develop a rich emotional vocabulary to accurately describe your experiences. An emotional vocabulary chart can aid self-awareness, uncovering patterns and promoting a deeper understanding.

Express Your Emotions:

Communicate emotions maturely. Shift from accusatory language ("You made me angry") to perceptual language

("I feel angry"). This fosters healthier communication, minimizing blame and empowering personal control.

Allow Others Their Emotions:

Establishing emotional boundaries enables you to detach from others' emotional experiences. Recognize that individuals are responsible for their emotions. This clarity leads to more fulfilling relationships.

OVERCOMING CODEPENDENCY

From a young age, I battled insecurity and low self-worth, seeking approval from others to counteract my inner turmoil. The demise of my parents' marriage during adolescence intensified my struggles, leaving me feeling like an island. In an attempt to counter negativity, I sought external validation, leading to a decade-long struggle with codependency.

My first codependent relationship, with an older cocaine addict, was marked by unhealthy routines, financial recklessness, and emotional abuse. His belittling and criticism fueled my belief in being incomplete and in need of repair. Fear-based behaviors emerged—obsession, control, and jealousy. After ten months, I summoned the courage to end this damaging relationship.

However, the codependent patterns persisted in subsequent relationships. A four-year stint with an alcoholic partner oscillated between love and violent fights. Seeking comfort after its end, I embraced another partner incapable of providing stability.

Upon realizing the destructive cycle, I faced myself and embarked on a journey of recovery. Alone in a new apartment, I sought help and turned to Melody Beattie's "Codependent No More." This transformative book lifted a weight as I recognized my behaviors and emotions. A checklist provided clarity, asking questions like:

1. Do you feel responsible for other people's well-being, thoughts, and feelings?
2. Are you compelled to solve others' problems and take care of their needs?
3. Do you find it easier to express anger about injustices to others than to yourself?
4. Do you feel safest and most comfortable when giving to others?
5. Do you feel insecure and guilty when receiving help?
6. Do you feel empty without someone to take care of or a crisis to manage?
7. Do you struggle to stop thinking about others' problems?
8. Do you lose interest in your own life when in love?
9. Do you stay in relationships, even if they don't work, to maintain love?

10. Do you leave bad relationships only to enter new ones that also don't work?

After nearly a decade of codependency, I faced my struggles, sought help, and embraced the path to recovery. Recognizing and understanding these patterns were crucial steps toward spiritual and emotional growth.

The most significant things I learned on this journey are:

Without change, nothing changes:

Embracing change is essential for breaking free from the cycle of codependency. Establishing a loving relationship with oneself is crucial for overcoming codependent patterns. Continually engaging in unhealthy relationships without self-love and growth will yield the same unsatisfactory results.

We can't control others, and it is not our job to do so:

Attempting to control and micromanage others, often manifested in choosing partners with dependencies, is a futile effort to escape one's negative feelings. Surrendering the need to control allows for the necessary space to connect with oneself. Recognizing that we can't control others provides the opportunity to focus on personal growth.

Love and obsessions are not the same:

Distinguishing between healthy love and obsession is crucial. The misconception that giving excessively to partners equates to happiness is debunked. Healthy love involves maintaining individual identities outside the romantic relationship, allowing both partners the freedom to pursue personal interests and projects. Prioritizing self-love rituals and activities fosters healing.

Life is not an emergency:

Living in a perpetual state of fear and stress, often centered on external factors beyond one's control, is detrimental. Recognizing that life is meant to be enjoyed and savored is key. Balancing a centered and focused heart helps navigate obstacles. Embracing each moment, accepting life's uncertainties, and trusting oneself or the Universe fosters a more enjoyable and fear-free existence.

CHAPTER 3

STOP OVERTHINKING

Overthinking doesn't sound so bad on the surface – thinking is good, right? But overthinking can cause problems. Here are some strategies to overcome it:

Awareness is the beginning of change:

Be aware of overthinking when it happens. Recognize the moments of doubt, stress, or anxiety, and use that awareness as the starting point for change.

Don't think of what can go wrong, but what can go right:

Overthinking is often fueled by fear. Instead of focusing on negative outcomes, visualize the positive possibilities. Keep thoughts about what can go right at the forefront of your mind.

Distract yourself into happiness:

Engage in positive, healthy activities to distract yourself from overanalysis. Activities like meditation, dancing, exercise, learning an instrument, or creative pursuits can shift your focus away from negative thoughts.

Put things into perspective:

Challenge the tendency to magnify issues. Ask yourself how much the situation will matter in the long term, whether it's in five years or a month. Putting things into perspective can help prevent overthinking.

Stop waiting for perfection:

Avoid the pursuit of perfection, which can be unrealistic and debilitating. Instead of waiting for perfect conditions, focus on making progress. Understand that waiting for perfection is not as smart as taking steps forward.

Change your view of fear:

Recognize that fear, often a root cause of overthinking, doesn't have to dictate outcomes. Every opportunity is a chance for a new beginning. Failure in the past doesn't guarantee failure in the future.

Put a timer to work:

Set specific time limits for overthinking. Allocate a short period to think, worry, and analyze, and then transition to a productive activity. Writing down concerns on paper during this time can also help release them.

Realize you can't predict the future:

Accept the uncertainty of the future. Spending excessive time worrying about it is unproductive. Focus on the present moment and engage in activities that bring joy and fulfillment.

Accept your best:

Overthinking is often rooted in feelings of inadequacy. Once you've given your best effort, accept it as such. Understand that success may involve factors beyond your control, and acknowledge your contributions.

Be grateful:

Cultivate gratitude by making lists of things you are thankful for. Gratitude shifts your focus from regretful or negative thoughts to positive aspects of your life. Sharing gratitude lists with a friend can enhance the experience.

Overthinking is a common challenge, but implementing these strategies can help transform it into a more positive, productive, and effective thought process.

OVERCOMING RUMINATION

Ever find yourself caught in a loop of repetitive thoughts, unable to break free? That's rumination – a mental pattern that can keep us stuck in the past or worrying about the future. But fear not, because breaking free from rumination is not only possible but also essential for a healthier mind.

Rumination is like a broken record playing the same tune over and over in our minds. It involves obsessively focusing on negative thoughts, replaying past events, or worrying about what might happen in the future. It's as if our minds get stuck in a loop, preventing us from moving forward.

Imagine rumination as a whirlpool that pulls us into a sea of negativity. The more we ruminate, the stronger the currents become, making it difficult to swim to calmer waters. This harmful cycle can lead to increased stress, anxiety, and a sense of helplessness. Breaking free from this cycle is crucial for our mental well-being.

The first step in overcoming rumination is recognizing the signs. It's like spotting dark clouds on the horizon – an indication that a storm might be coming. Common signs of rumination include repetitive thoughts, excessive self-criticism, and a persistent focus on problems without finding solutions. By becoming aware of these signs, we can take proactive steps to intervene.

Mindfulness: Bringing Back the Present

Mindfulness is like a gentle anchor that helps us stay grounded in the present moment. When we're caught up in rumination, our minds are often dwelling on the past or worrying about the future. Mindfulness involves paying attention to the here and now – observing our thoughts without judgment. It's like stepping out of the whirlpool and onto solid ground.

Breaking the Thought Loop

Imagine your thoughts as a train moving along a track. Rumination is like the train getting stuck in a loop, circling the same negative thoughts. Breaking the thought loop involves redirecting the train onto a new track. When negative thoughts arise, consciously choose to shift your focus to something positive or engage in an activity that brings joy. It's a small but powerful step towards breaking free from the repetitive cycle.

Setting Boundaries with Worry

Worrying is like a persistent visitor knocking on our mental door. While some worries are valid, excessive worrying can fuel rumination. Setting boundaries with worry involves allocating specific time slots to address concerns. It's like telling the worry visitor, "I'll listen to you, but only during our scheduled appointment." This helps prevent intrusive worries from taking over our thoughts throughout the day.

Problem-Solving: Turning Thoughts into Actions

Rumination often involves dwelling on problems without finding solutions. Problem-solving is like turning the wheel of a ship, steering us away from the storm. When faced with a challenge, break it down into smaller, manageable steps. Take action on what you can control and accept what you can't. This proactive approach transforms rumination into constructive problem-solving.

Cultivating a Gratitude Practice

Gratitude is like sunshine breaking through the clouds of negativity. Cultivating a gratitude practice involves regularly reflecting on the positive aspects of our lives. It's not about denying difficulties but shifting our focus to what we appreciate. Writing down three things we're grateful for each day is a simple yet effective way to break the grip of rumination.

Engaging in Purposeful Activities

Imagine rumination as a fog that obscures our vision. Engaging in purposeful activities is like a gust of wind that clears the fog. Pursue activities that bring joy, meaning, and a sense of accomplishment. It could be a hobby, spending time with loved ones, or contributing to a cause. These activities disrupt the rumination cycle and create positive momentum.

Overcoming rumination is a gradual process that involves cultivating awareness, practicing mindfulness, and taking proactive steps to shift our mental patterns. By recognizing the signs, embracing mindfulness, breaking the thought loop, setting boundaries with worry, and engaging in purposeful activities, we can break free from the cycle of rumination. rumination brings us closer to a healthier, more balanced mind.

It's natural for our moods to fluctuate, and everyone experiences highs and lows. While our mood can significantly influence our perspective and behavior, it's essential to strike a balance and not let it become the sole determining factor in how we approach life. Here are some considerations:

1. Label Your Emotions

Acknowledge and label your emotions accurately. Identify whether you're feeling nervous, disappointed, sad, or another emotion. Sometimes, anger may mask more vulnerable emotions like shame or embarrassment, so dig deeper. Naming your emotions helps take the sting out of them and allows you to understand their potential impact on your decisions.

2. Reframe Your Thoughts

Recognize how your emotions influence your perception of events. Reframe your thoughts to develop a more realistic view of situations. Challenge negative thoughts and consider alternative, positive perspectives. Imagine what advice you would give to a friend facing a similar situation. Changing the emotional filter through which you view the world can lead to more rational thinking.

3. Engage in a Mood Booster

Break the cycle of a bad mood by actively engaging in activities that boost your spirits. Avoid negative behaviors like isolating yourself or mindlessly scrolling through your phone. Instead, do things that typically bring you joy or happiness. Call a friend to discuss positive topics, go for a walk, meditate, listen to uplifting music, or engage in activities that you enjoy.

Additional Tips

- Address emotional wounds rather than suppressing them, as unattended emotions can worsen over time.

- Acknowledge your feelings without letting them control you.

- Take control of your mood and turn your day around by making proactive choices.

- Recognize that managing emotions is not about suppressing them but about gaining control over them.

- Practice emotional regulation consistently to build mental strength.

Remember, managing emotions is a skill that requires practice and dedication. By implementing these strategies, you can become more adept at regulating your emotions and fostering mental strength.

At times, we all wonder if we're doing enough, earning enough, or achieving "success." I know this well, having spent much of my early adulthood in a constant state of fear and self-doubt.

After college, I worked long hours in a corporate job, thinking it meant success, though it wasn't what I truly wanted. I clung to dead-end jobs, toxic relationships, and draining friendships, fearing I'd be seen as a quitter if I left them.

My decisions were based on others' desires, not my own. Constantly grappling with confidence and second-guessing myself, I realized the "woe is me" mindset can be crippling if not addressed promptly.

Here are a few things I've learned to combat self-doubt and boost confidence, which might help you too:

Quit Comparing:

Stop comparing your achievements to others'. I doubted myself most when measuring my accomplishments against others'. Remember, everyone is on their unique journey. Success lies in following what works for you, even if it differs from those you admire.

Ignore Others' Opinions:

Don't worry about what others think. Focusing on others' opinions holds you back. To pursue your dreams, release the need for approval. Otherwise, you'll be trapped in constant self-doubt.

Decide and Adjust:

Don't dwell on decisions; overthinking fuels self-doubt. Trust your initial instinct, as it comes from intuition rather than ego. Make a decision, then adjust your course as needed. Remember, "no feeling is final," and the same applies to decisions.

Pen a Personal Letter:

When feeling down and without external support, turn to the one person who can always lift you—yourself. A beneficial practice I've developed is writing a hand-written letter to myself. Acknowledge the shadow side—the negative, doubtful, scared part—and let the light side—the positive, optimistic, and productive self—reassure. List recent accomplishments to boost confidence. (It truly works!)

Practice Gratitude Every Evening:

Instead of dwelling on what's lacking, focus on what you have and have achieved. Maintain a gratitude journal, reflecting on the day's positives. Investing energy in gratitude creates a positive mindset, leading to good feelings. When you feel positive, good things tend to happen.

Cherish Supportive Relationships:

No one succeeds alone. Identify your biggest fans—those who consistently uplift and reassure you. Friends, family, and peers who see your greatness. Nurture these relationships, drawing strength and confidence from them. Recognize their support as a valuable asset.

Lean on Mantras for Strength:

Develop a set of personal mantras to combat self-doubt. Repeat them when doubt creeps in, reminding yourself of your progress and worth. One example: "You are loved." Combat feelings of inadequacy by reinforcing the knowledge that you are surrounded by love and support. This practice minimizes self-doubt by deepening your experience of love.

CHAPTER 4

CREATING A LOVELY LIFE

Life is comparable to a grand painting, and in this chapter, we'll explore how to craft it into a masterpiece. It's not about achieving perfection but about fostering joy and maintaining resilience during challenges.

Fostering Positivity

Envision sunshine warming your heart; that's the essence of positivity. It enhances your days and fills your world with cheerful hues. It doesn't mean overlooking challenges but facing them with a smile, confident that things will improve.

Begin each day by expressing gratitude for the positives—like a comforting cup of cocoa, a friendly greeting, or the sun breaking through clouds. Thankfulness helps you find the silver lining even in tough times.

Words carry immense power. Use affirming words about yourself daily, such as "I am strong" or "I can handle challenges." These words cultivate inner courage.

Consider your friends—are they positive and supportive? If so, spend time with them, share your dreams, and let them uplift you. Extend kindness to others to build a circle of happy friends.

Life is akin to learning to ride a bike; you may stumble, but you rise and try again. View challenges as opportunities for learning and growth, shaping a better version of yourself.#

Life is hectic, but take occasional breaks. Close your eyes, inhale deeply, and simply be present. It promotes a sense of calm and happiness.

Celebrate your achievements, no matter how small. Recognition fuels positive feelings and motivates you to do more good things.

Cultivating Resilience

Resilience is akin to the strength of a tree that bends but doesn't break in the wind. It's about getting up when life knocks you down.

Life is full of surprises, so embrace changes. Just as in playing with toys, sometimes you alter the game. Accepting change facilitates learning new things.

When things don't go as planned, don't perceive it as failure; see it as an opportunity to learn and improve.

Problem-solving is akin to assembling a puzzle. Break it into smaller pieces, find solutions, and try again. This iterative process enhances your ability to overcome challenges.

Friends and family form a supportive team. When faced with problems, share them. They offer comfort and creative solutions.

Be kind to yourself. If times are tough, it's okay. Everyone encounters challenges. Treat yourself with compassion, remembering that you're doing your best.

Maintain a strong body through good food, sufficient sleep, and engaging in activities you love. A robust body supports a resilient mind.

Certain things are beyond control, like the weather. Focus on what you can control—it fosters strength and happiness.

Building a Beautiful Life: A Harmonious Blend

Life is akin to a joyous dance, where positivity is the uplifting music and resilience are the sturdy steps that keep you moving even when the melody changes.

Imagine your life as a grand puzzle—positivity provides the vibrant pieces, and resilience is how they interlock, creating a picture of a happy and resilient you.

Craft a space filled with joy—vibrant colors, positive people, and good vibes. This nurtures inner well-being and contributes to personal growth.

Envision things you wish to achieve. Positivity instills belief, and resilience sustains your effort even in challenging times.

Life is a school of learning; positivity makes it enjoyable, and resilience prevents you from giving up when faced with difficulty. Every challenge is an opportunity to acquire new knowledge.

Being happy is akin to possessing a radiant light. Share your joy with others through kindness and assistance. This transforms the world into a more beautiful place for everyone.

So, building a beautiful life is akin to painting with joyful colors. Be grateful, stay strong, and recognize that even small steps contribute to a magnificent life portrait.

HOW TO RECONNECT AND START LOVING YOURSELF

We often criticize ourselves, and it's common to put ourselves down without feeling guilty about prioritizing others.

Without realizing it, we have negative thoughts about ourselves, doubting our abilities and worth. We don't question this habit, constantly sabotaging ourselves as a form of self-protection.

This leads to an ongoing internal struggle. Hearing aggressive and toxic thoughts about ourselves feels unnatural and creates a constant battle within.

To overcome this, making peace with yourself should be your top priority. Focus on self-improvement before anything else. Success in relationships, career, and life starts with being successful with yourself.

So, how can you achieve inner peace and start loving yourself?

1. Developing Awareness in Your Thoughts

Do you truly know yourself? Are you mindful of the thoughts that enter your mind? If not, begin to increase your focus. Concentrate on your thoughts; don't divert your attention to the weather, colleagues, classmates, friends, or family. Right now, pay attention to the thoughts you're allowing into yourself.

Keep focusing. Don't give up just yet. Continuing may be challenging, but the rewards are worth it.

Now that you're becoming aware of the thoughts nourishing your mind, body, and spirit, take action.

How do you act when everything is happening within yourself? Shift the game in your favor. Become the master of your thoughts, emotions, and feelings. Show your autopilot brain who's in charge.

To achieve that, enhance your focusing power. Train your brain to follow your lead. Be warned—it won't let you dominate it easily. You'll face initial struggles. The key is, whenever you notice a negative, self-destructive thought about your internal self or external environment, immediately instruct your brain to switch thoughts. Update the operating system. Replace the negative thought with a positive one.

While many advocate for having a monologue with yourself, engaging in a dialogue is even better. Speak to yourself as you would to someone you genuinely love. Treat yourself as your best friend.

Consistently and constantly implement this habit every day. You'll be amazed at the changes within and outside yourself. You'll become more empathetic, open, and outgoing with others. Making friends will be easier, and you'll adapt to any person without being judgmental or condescending. You'll radiate light.

2. Enhancing Self-Awareness in Body Language

Did you know that 96% of what we convey isn't through words? This means the majority happens beyond what you say. Your body possesses its own language, speaking volumes to both yourself and others.

Direct your attention to your body. What does your posture convey right now? What message do you want your body to communicate to yourself and others? Train your body to follow your lead. Learn to command your body language.

Every detail matters. From your stance to your smile, you are constantly conveying who you are to yourself and those around you. Open arms and a raised head signal openness to yourself, others, and the universe.

You might notice low-power postures. Swiftly replace these with high-power postures. Carry yourself in the manner you wish to be perceived. Continually ask yourself: How would the person I aspire to become present themselves right now?

If you desire confidence and positivity, position yourself as a confident and positive individual. Avoiding eye contact and always looking down signals discomfort with yourself and others, making it difficult for others to take you seriously.

To earn respect from others, start by respecting yourself. It begins with how your body communicates about you. Never underestimate the impact of body language, your voice tone, your walk, and your gestures. Every aspect reveals something about you, and people will notice.

Get comfortable with your body, and it will collaborate with you, taking you wherever you want. Seeking confidence? Encourage your body to exude confidence.

3. Cherishing Alone Time

To truly understand yourself, there's a simple thing you should do: spend time alone. When you meet a stranger, you don't hesitate to spend hours discussing who they are, their interests, and their positive qualities. Why not do the same for yourself?

It's intriguing how we often prioritize others over ourselves, believing they are more deserving of our time. Isn't that surprising?

Allocate at least 30 minutes each day to be with yourself. No one else. No external distractions. You should always have this intimate connection with your inner self, regardless of your location or company. Nothing and no one should interfere with that.

I appreciate how Tim Groover talks about being in the "zone." You should always be in your zone—no external distractions, just you focused on what matters most at the moment. The person closest to you should always be yourself. Otherwise, you give someone outside of you too much influence over your feelings, actions, and experiences.

People may label you as selfish or egotistic, but they often say this because they feel discontented themselves. Attaining a higher level of consciousness is crucial to recognizing the significance of being close to yourself.

You can't truly thrive and support others if you neglect yourself. To give love to others, you must first give love to yourself. In my perspective, this is an unwavering principle.

5. Eliminate Negativity

This is crucial. If you aim to rejuvenate yourself and become a healthy, positive, and resilient individual, you must remove all toxic elements from your life.

These could be a job, a friend, unhealthy food, bad habits, or a family member draining the life out of you. Anything that pulls you down, cut it out.

I want to emphasize an important point, though. There will be challenging times in your life, as there are for everyone, where cutting people out might not be feasible. There will be instances when the people you love the most are going through tough times, and you'll need to support them.

Being a sensitive person, I understand how challenging it can be not to absorb the energies and vibrations of those you love. However, with a lot of effort and focus, it's absolutely possible. Remind yourself every day that drowning in these negative emotions isn't helping you, and it's not helping the people you care about.

Always take some distance and consider the bigger picture.

CONCLUSION

As we reach the end of this journey together, I hope the pages of "How To Let Go Of Past Trauma and Make Peace With Yourself" have been a guiding light on your path to healing. Reflecting on the exploration of forgiveness, emotional freedom, and the creation of a more beautiful life, remember that this is not just a book; it's a companion on your personal journey toward peace.

Your journey is unique, filled with twists and turns, victories, and challenges. Embracing the process of letting go is a courageous step toward self-discovery and emotional well-being. Whether you found solace in the practical exercises, comfort in shared experiences, or inspiration in the possibility of a brighter future, know that every small insight gained contributes to your growth.

As you move forward, consider the power of positivity in shaping your reality. Life is a canvas waiting for your strokes of joy and resilience. Each day is an opportunity to add vibrant hues to the masterpiece of your existence. The simple steps outlined in these pages are tools for you to reclaim your agency, fostering a sense of beauty and fulfillment.

If this book has resonated with you, I encourage you to share your thoughts. Leaving a positive review and rating is not just a way to express gratitude; it's an act of kindness that helps others discover the potential for healing within these words. Your words may be the encouragement someone else needs to embark on their journey to letting go and finding peace.

Thank you for entrusting me with a small part of your journey. It has been an honor to walk alongside you through the exploration of past traumas and the pursuit of a more beautiful life. As you take these lessons forward, may your days be filled with moments of peace, joy, and the unwavering belief in the strength that resides within you.

Printed in Great Britain
by Amazon

38239863R00036